COUNTRY SONGS
of faith, hope & love

ISBN-13: 978-1-4234-2268-6
ISBN-10: 1-4234-2268-6

HAL•LEONARD®
CORPORATION

7777 W. BLUEMOUND RD. P.O. BOX 13819 MILWAUKEE, WI 53213

Visit Hal Leonard Online at
www.halleonard.com

ANGELS AMONG US

Words and Music by BECKY HOBBS
and DON GOODMAN

6

sent down to us from some-where up a-bove. _ They come to

you and me _ in our dark-est hours _ to

show us how to live, _ to teach us how to give, _ to

guide us with the light of _ love.

BLESS THE BROKEN ROAD

Words and Music by MARCUS HUMMON,
BOBBY BOYD and JEFF HANNA

D.S. al Coda

-ken road _____ that led me straight ___

to you.

BELIEVE

Words and Music by RONNIE DUNN
and CRAIG WISEMAN

Moderately slow

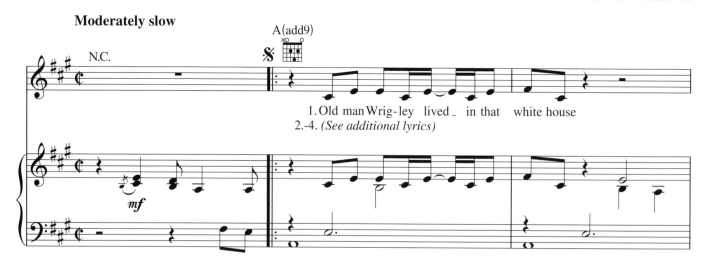

1. Old man Wrig-ley lived in that white house
2.-4. *(See additional lyrics)*

down the street where I grew up. Ma-ma used to send

me o-ver with things. We struck a friend - ship up.

Additional Lyrics

2. Said he was in the war, went in the Navy,
   Lost his wife, lost his baby.
   Broke down and asked him one time:
   "How you keep from goin' crazy?"
   He said, "I'll see my wife and son in just a little while."
   I asked him what he meant, he looked at me and smiled,
   Refrain

3. A few years later I was off at college,
   Talking to Mom on the phone one night.
   Gettin' all caught up on the gossip,
   The ins and outs of the small town life.
   She said, "Oh, by the way, son, Old Man Wrigley's died."

4. Later on that night,
   I laid there thinkin' back.
   'Thought a couple long lost summers,
   I didn't know whether to cry or laugh.
   If there was ever anybody
   'Deserved a ticket to the other side,
   It'd be that sweet old man [who]
   Looked me in the eye,
   Refrain

BLESSED

Words and Music by BRETT JAMES,
HILLARY LINDSEY and TROY VERGES

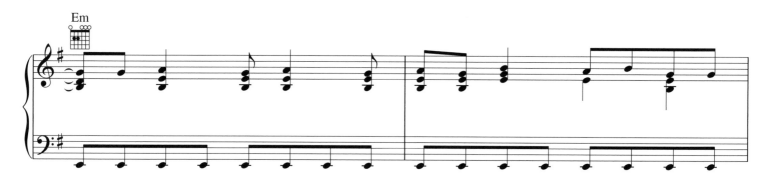

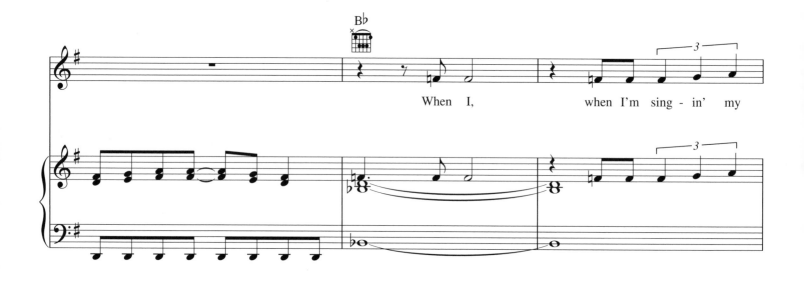

When I, when I'm sing - in' my

kids to sleep, ___ when I feel you hold - in' me, ___

FACE OF GOD

Words and Music by TOM SHAPIRO,
BOB DiPIERO and RIVERS RUTHERFORD

GOD'S WILL

Words and Music by TOM DOUGLAS
and BARRY DEAN

Moderately slow

I met God's Will on a Hal-low-een night, he was dressed as a bag of leaves.

It hid the brac-es on his legs at first.

His smile was as bright as the Au-gust sun when he looked at me.

* Recorded a half step lower.

HOLES IN THE FLOOR OF HEAVEN

Words and Music by WILLIAM A. KIRSCH
and STEVE WARINER

Moderately slow

One day shy __ of eight __ years old __ when
Sea - sons come __ and sea - sons go, __
lit - tle girl __ is twen - ty - three, __ I

Grand - ma passed __ a - way,
noth - ing stays __ the same.
walk her down __ the aisle.

I was a bro - ken - heart - ed lit -
I grew up, __
It's a shame her mom __ can't be __

- tle boy, __ blow - ing out that birth - day cake. __
fell in love, __ met a girl who took __ my name. __
__ here now __ to see her love - ly smile. __

* Recorded a half step lower.

watch - ing o - ver you ___ and ___ me. ___

Well, my

I HOPE YOU DANCE

Words and Music by TIA SILLERS
and MARK D. SANDERS

I NEED YOU

Words and Music by DENNIS MATKOSKY
and TY LACY

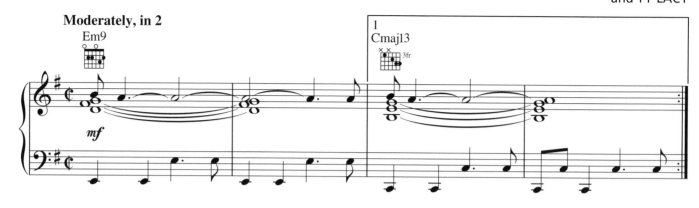

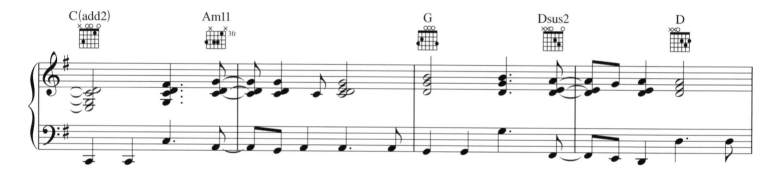

I don't need a lot ___ of things; I can

Vocal line written one octave higher than sung.

car - ries me ___ through. ___ I need You. ___

You're the hope that moves ___ me to

I WANT TO STROLL OVER HEAVEN WITH YOU

Words and Music by
J.B. LEMLEY

D.S. al Coda

So man - y

CODA

I want to stroll ___ o - ver heav - en ___ with ___

you.

rit.

IN GOD WE STILL TRUST

Words and Music by KIM NASH,
BILL NASH and ROBERT LeCLAIR

* *Recorded a half step lower.*

LOVE CAN CHANGE YOUR MIND

Words and Music by BOB FARRELL
and REGIE HAMM

an - gels __ had flown __ a - way. __ But now __ my

heart has __ come home __ and I know __ that it's here __ to

stay, oh, 'cause love can __ change __ your mind, __

whoa. __

JESUS TAKE THE WHEEL

Words and Music by BRETT JAMES,
GORDIE SAMPSON and HILLARY LINDSEY

LONG BLACK TRAIN

Words and Music by
JOSH TURNER

Moderate Country Gospel

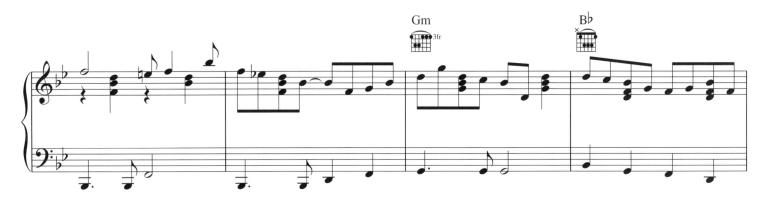

D.S. al Coda

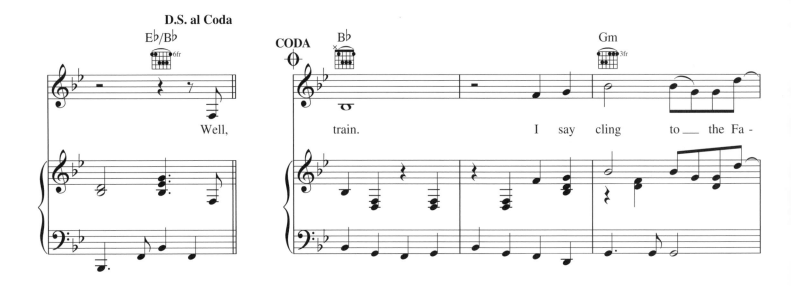

Well,

CODA

train.   I   say   cling   to ___ the Fa -

LOVE CAN BUILD A BRIDGE

Words and Music by PAUL OVERSTREET,
JOHN JARVIS and NAOMI JUDD

ONE VOICE

Words and Music by DON COOK
and DAVID MALLOY

Some kids have and some _ kids don't, and some of us _ are won-der-ing why. _
house, a yard, a neigh - bor-hood where you could ride _ your new bike to school. _

And Mom won't watch the news _ at night; _ there's _ too much stuff that's mak-ing her cry. _
A kind - a world where Mom _ and Dad _____ still be - lieve the gold - en rule. _

We need _ some help _
Life's not _ that sim - ple _
(D.S.) Thanks for _ the help _

THIS IS GOD

Words and Music by
PHIL VASSAR

Hey, this is God. _ Could I please _ have your at - ten - tion.

There's a need _ for in - ter - ven - tion. Man, _ I'm dis - ap - point - ed in what I'm see - in'.

Yeah, this is God. _ You fight each oth - er in _ my name. _

WHEN I GET WHERE I'M GOIN'

Words and Music by RIVERS RUTHERFORD
and GEORGE TEREN

THREE WOODEN CROSSES

Words and Music by KIM WILLIAMS
and DOUG JOHNSON

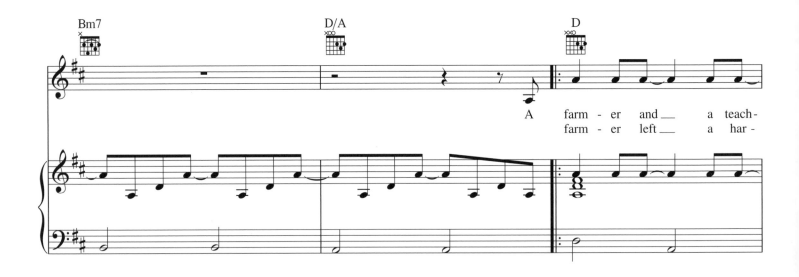

A farm-er and ___ a teach-
farm-er left ___ a har-

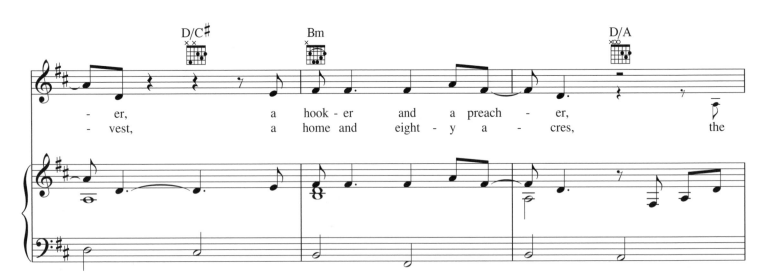

-er, a hook-er and a preach-er,
-vest, a home and eight-y a-cres, the

Recorded a half step lower.

WHERE WERE YOU
(When the World Stopped Turning)

Words and Music by
ALAN JACKSON

some kind __ of an-swer   and   look   at   your-self __   and   what   real - ly   mat - ters?
mov - ie _____ you're watch-in'   and

I'm   just   a   sing - er   of __   sim - ple   songs. __   I'm   not   a

real   po - lit - i - cal __   man.   I   watch   C - N - N, __   but   I'm   not __

__ sure   I   can   tell   you   the   dif - f'rence   in   I - raq   and   I - ran.   But

WHAT IF SHE'S AN ANGEL

Words and Music by
BRYAN WAYNE

know-in' deep down it could-'ve been her ___ sav - in' grace. ___

What if she's an an - gel?

rit.